ENGLISH-SVANETIAN DICTIONARY

by

Oliver Wardrop

Sir O. Wardrop, *English-Svanetian Dictionay*, Journal of the Royal Asiatic Society 1911, XVI, 589-634.

Copyright © 2018 acad.ge

ISBN: 99419616
ISBN-13: 978-9941-96-1-6

INTRODUCTION

THE recent establishment of a fund in the University of Oxford for the encouragement of the study of the Georgian family of languages may in the course of time attract the attention of British philologists to the Western Caucasus, and an increasing stream of travelers will doubtless find their way thither seeking knowledge, health, sport, and scenery; it is for such visitors that the following vocabulary has been compiled. More than twenty years ago the late Mr. D. Peacock included Svanetian among the five languages of which he published vocabularies in the Journal of the Royal Asiatic Society, but the material was scanty, and a large number of errors are to be found in it. Most of the books on the subject are in Russian, and the script into which the Svanetian words are transliterated is troublesome and is inconsistently used. What is required is an exact record of the spoken language by means of the phonograph, and it is to be hoped that some British student may undertake the task before long. All that is attempted here is to give a starting-point for serious study. As many forms as possible have been included, and no attempt has been made to distinguish the dialects of Upper and Lower Svanetia. The spelling is phonetic as far as may be. The abbreviation G. shows that there are Georgian words strikingly similar, and generally, though not always, having the same meaning; many of such words are borrowed by the Georgian from other languages.

The following bibliographical note may be useful, though it does not claim to be by any means a complete list of the books on the subject:

1. *Lushnu Anban, Svanetskaya Azbulca.* Tiflis, 1804.

Published by the Society for the Propagation of Christianity in the Caucasus. Baron Uslar is believed to be its author. It is still a most useful book to a student of the language, but copies are rare. Among its merits may be mentioned the Georgian translation of every word, as well as the Russian. It gives several specimens of the language in the form of prayers, Bible history, and a few phrases.

2. *Vol. X of Sbornik materialov dlya opisaniya Kavkaza,* containing four lists of words collected by I. Nizharadze (himself a Svanetian), M. Zavadskii, A. Stoyanov, and A. Gren;

the systems of transliteration employed are inconsistent and irritating. There are also ethnographical, statistical, and other sketches, folk-tales, folk-songs with music, etc.

3. The Proceedings (Trudy) of the Fifth Archaeological Congress, Tiflis, 1881, with an article by A. I. Stoyanov.

4. A. Tsagareli, *0 grammaticheskoi literaturie gruzinskago yazyka.* St. Petersburg, 1878. pp. 70-9 and 81.

5. A. Tsagareli, *Sravnitelnii Obzor morfologii.* St. Petersburg, 1872 (lithographed).

6. Uslar, in vol. ix. of *Shornik svedenii o kavkazskieh gortsakh,* p. 4.

The above are only of use to those who read Russian.

7. Rosen, *Ueber das Mingrelische, Sua'nische, u. Abchasische.*

8. Fr. Bopp, *Die Kaukasischen Glieder des Indo-Europae-ischen Sprachstamms.* Berlin, 1847.

9. Max Müller, *Languages* of the Seat of *War,* p. 114.

10. Ferd. Bork, *Kaukasische Miscellen.* Königsberg, 1907.

11. R. von Erckert, *Die Sprachen des Kaukasischen Stammes.* Wien, 1895.

12. D. Peacock, *Original Vocabularies of Five West Caucasian Languages*: JRAS., Vol. XIX, Pt. I, 1887.

13. G. Radde's *Reisen (v. infra)*, on pp. 84-91, contains a vocabulary.

The. following authors of works relating to Svanetia, but not dealing especially with the language, may be mentioned: D. Freshfield, Mummery, C. Phillips-Woolley, von Dechy, Merzbacher, Nadiezhdin, Dubrovin, Gamrekeli, Mamatsov, Nemirovich-Danchenko, Shakhovskoi, Bartolomaei, Dobrovolskii, Gilev, K. A. Borozdin, Gabriel Cicodze (late Bishop of Imeretia). D. Bakradze (in vol. vi, 1867, of Memoirs of Caucasian Section of Russ. Geog. Soc., in Nos. 1, 2, and 4 of newspaper *Kavkaz* for 1867 and Nos. 59, 77, and 80 of *Kavkaz* for 1877: also reprinted at Tiflis in 1877 as a small pamphlet of 37 pages), A. I. Stoyanov (in vol. x of Memoirs of Caucasian Section of' Russ. Geog. Soc., pp. 289-472, Tifiis, 1876 - travels, topography, etc.), G. Radde (in vol. vii, 1868, of Memoirs of Caucasian Section of Russ. Geog. Soc., 222 pp., chiefly biological and geographical, being a Russian translation of *Reisen im Mingrelischcn Hochgebirge*, Tifiis, 1866, with three maps and nine plates in separate atlas in 4to), R. Bernoville *(La Souanethie libre*, Paris, 1875, 4to, 181 pp., with seven plates, illustrations in text, and map - chiefly historical and ethnographical), G. D. Filimonov (in *Viestnik* of Society of Ancient Russian Art, Moscow, 1870 - archaeology), M. Kovalevsky's *Law and Custom in the Caucasus* (Moscow, 1890), and numerous articles in the Georgian and other newspapers and periodicals of Transcaucasia.

The late Miss Marjory Wardrop left in manuscript An English translation of a collection of Svanetian folk-tales which may be published shortly.

ENGLISH-SVANETIAN VOCABULARY

A

Able (to be), *liimade, libets*; I can, *mi mibits*; thou canst, *si dchibits*; he
can, *achas khobits* ; I could, *maymada*: thou couldst, *dchaymada*; he
could, *khaymada*; he was able to bring water, *achas khaymada nitsi
likhde.*

Abode, *lalzigal (lizge, to live), sadgem* (G. sadyomi).

Accompany (to), *linkhri.*

Account, reckoning, *angiarish* (G. angarishi).

Acorn, *shgvib.*

Advantage, *lisargebel* (G.).

Afterwards, *echungho, achungho, amungho.*

Again, *dchuad, adjagh, zhiid.*

Agree (to), *lit'hankhme* (G. dat'hankmeba).

Aim, target, *nishani* (G.); to take aim, *limtzuina, Unshani*;
he

  aimed, *lekhmctsuna.*

Air, *haier* (G. haeri).

Alarm : do not (thou) be alarmed ! *ghanunp'hesheni.*

Alder *(Alnus incana), balqacl, bölkösh.*

All, *mag, mak, chi, chie:* more than all, *chid, chinmashenam.*

Allow (to), *limbe, likhvie*; he allowed, *kat'hnebe* (G.);
allow

  me! (sing.), *khakhvi.*

Alms (to give), *limkheeri.*

Alpenstock, *midchvra, mudchvra, mudchru, pawu.*

Already, *ser.*

Altogether, *hadurd, mchad.*

Always, *chigar, chigarmek.*

Ambush, *lipezh, lalp'har* (G. *sap'hari*).

Amusing, *lasht'hbin*.

Ancient, *dzghydkhanishli* (cf. G. *didkhan*), *djuvel* (? cf. G. *dzveli*).

And, *i*.

Angry (to be), *likhtsi, list'hike, litsral*: he was angry, *adsest'hke*.

Animal, *kuinlymgene, piryutkh* (beast) (G.); *tzkhovel* (living thing) (G.).

Ankle, *purskal*.

Annual, yearly, *luza* (cf. *za*, year).

Another, *ishgen*.

Answer (to), *lipsukhe* (G. *pasukheba*).

Ant, *dchindchvil* (G. *dchindchvela*), *morshk, myshk*.

Anvil, *kvadch*.

Appear (to), it appears, *esrenish*.

Apple, apple-tree, *visgv, vusgv, vusk* (G. *vashli*).

Archangel, *t'hargrezer, t'harigzela, t'harigdzeva*. (G. *mt'hava-rangelozi*).

Arm, *mekhar* (G. *mkhari*).

Arms, weapons, *havedch* (G. *avedchi*, household goods, furniture).

Army, *lashgar* (G. *lashkari*).

Around, *girkid*.

Arrive (to), *likhed, lizi, liqed*; he arrived, *emquedi, anqad, at'hqedun*; he has arrived, *lakhagan*; they arrived, *anqadkh*.

Arrow, *tsku, tskhui, tzukhend*.

Artisan, *ostat* (G.).

As if, *mugvda*.

Ascent, slope, *lamlezha, lamelzha*.

Ashamed (to be), *lishgve*.

Ashes, *tyt*.

Ask (to), *lidched, likural, likhir, lishguem*: ask! (thou), *isgala- khuran*.

Aspen, *yerlchv* (G. *verkhvi*), *elkhvra*.

Ass, *tsel, tsanika*; she-ass, *dchak tsel*, i.e. mare-ass (cf. horse); foal of an ass, *tseli sabel*.

Assembly, *korvan* (caravan), *lalkhori, lakhor, lizvre*; to assemble, *linzore, lizvri, lilkhore*; they assembled, *adzu- renkh*; folk-moot, *djan nazuran, lukhor, luzor*; place of assembly, *lakhor*.

Astonish (to), *liskurelal*; to be astonished, *limhazhe*; he was astonished, *ambazhini, lakhumbazhan*.

Attack, *lishgeb*; to attack, *lidchvad*.

Aunt, *giga*.

Autumn, *muzhgura, muzhghver*.

Avarice, *litsingvil*.

Axe, *kada, kagda, nassol* (a large axe).

Azalea pontica, *hadra*.

Baby, *chindivlid.*

Bachelor, *uchizha, uchizhala.*

Back, *shiq, shikha, siki, chagar*; back of the neck, *qintchkh.*

Backside, posteriors, *sadrak.*

Backwards, *ghveshg, gheshgmav, gheshgmavghak, osh, osht'h, goshkht'h, gosht'h, oshkmagd, oshkmal, ueshkmal, uveshgmau.*

Bad, *khola, leg*; badly, *kholamd.*

Bag, *dzadzra* (sack); leathern bag, *katsi, khalt'ha.*

Baggage, load, *barg* (G.).

Bake (to), roast, *linqe.*

Bank, shore, *dzgid* (G. *cidè*).

Barberry, *gotskhir* (G. *cotsakhuri*).

Bare, naked, *metqop'he.*

Bark, rind, *tzil.*

Bark (to), *likhshde.*

Barley, *chomin, chemen* (cf. Russ.), *kere* (G. *keri*; cf. *Gerste* in German).

Barn, *kalv* (cf. G. *calo*).

Barrel, *sagomela*; small cask, *okhri.*

Basin, *tashd* (G. *tashti*).

Basket, *kuid, lashyq. Kuid* is a measure of 2 poods Russ.; *kuidol* (dim.) is half a pood; *leghvliak* one-third or one-fourth of a *kuid.* (Cf. M. Kovalevsky, vol. ii, p. 14 note; *gvidol (kuidol)* is 2 poods 17 lb. Russ.)

Bastard, *bush, byushv* (G. *bushi*).

Bat, *mat'hkhap'h* (G. *machkateli*).

Battle, *lizuriel.*

Be (to), *lirde, lide*: it is, *ari, li*; they are, *arikh*; thou art, *khi, khe*; we are, *khuid*; I was, *michde*; he was (Lat. *erat*), *arda*; they were, *erdekh, at'hasdakh*: he will be, *cri*; it will be, *ira, iri*.

Beads (string of), *dzivar* (G. *mdzivi*, bead).

Beak (of bird), *nisqart'hi, niskert* (G. *niscarti*).

Beam, joist, *dir, shdukhir*.

Beans, *rogv, rog, geder* (cf. peas).

Bear, *dasht'h, dashte, dashdv* (G. *datvi*).

Bear a child (to), *lit'hne* ; she bore, *akht'hanan*.

Bear fruit (to), *lishne* ; it bears fruit, *khashne*.

Beard, *ver* (G. *tsveri*), *vere, vare, chadsh, chardsh, lazpura*; bearded, luver.

Beast, *khets* (G. *mkhetzi*).

Beat (to), *liqer*; beat (thou) him ! *khatqatzdas*; beat ye him (or them)! *khakhidd*.

Beautiful, *sgvam, lamas* (G. *lamazi*), *musguen*.

Because, *adjghere*.

Bed, *taht*; bedding, *laqvra, lakura, lakhura, lerchal, lerkuali*; bed-cover, *saban* (G.), *shkartuin*; feather bed, *bumbyl* (G. *bumbuli*, down); to make a bed, *laqvrash lirshi*.

Bee, *mer, layhvba*.

Beech (Fagus sylvatica), tzipra *(Mingr.* tzipelli, G. tsipheli).

Beech forest, *letzp'her*.

Beef, *zer, leghv*.

Beer, *uorash*.

Before, in front, *zgvebin*.

Before, previously, *mankwi*.

Beg (to), entreat, *likhural*.

Begin (to), *libne*; I began, *akhuibin*; they began, *lagsihuds*;
from tbe beginning, first of all, *chiq*.

Behind, *veshgin*; from behind, *gheshkim*, *goshkin*,
ghoshgin.

Believe (to), *lijravi* (G. *jera*).

Bell, *zara* (G. *zar'i*); little bell, *rozhven* (G. *ezhvani*).

Belly, *kadil*, *kadu*, *khat'h*, *khad* (G. *cudchi*).

Below, beneath, *anchu*.

Belt, *lartq* (G. *sartqeli*); below the belt, beneath the waist,
lartq anchu.

Bench, seat, *sqam* (G., Lat.).

Better, *khochamd*, *makhecheni*; better than all, *chidmachene*,
chinmachene, *khecheni*.

Between: between the legs, *nabrakhs*.

Beyond, *qamchu*.

Big, *dzkhod* (G. *didi*), *khosha* (elder).

Bind (to), (cf. tether), *lildjeni*; he bound him (or them),
at'hlanj;

to hind up, bandage, *lit'hle*.

Birch-tree *(Betula alba)*, *zhachver*, *yokvra*, *yokver* (G.
arqi).

Bird, *nep'hal*, *nepol*, *napr*, *p'hrinvel* (G.); chick,
tzindav. Birth, *chvadguash*.

Bitch, *jua* (G. *dzucna*).

Bitter, *mykhim*, *myny*, *modzib* (G. *mtsare*, *mdzaghe*).

Bitterness, *limkhyme*.

Black, *mcshkhe*, *neshkhe*.

Blacksmith, *myshkid* (G. *mdchedeli*).

Bless (to), *lidjgry*, *limzyri*; blessed, *namzur*, *chot'hmezira*;
bless!

(imp. sing.), *chot'hmozurad* ; a blessing, *lamzur.*

Blind, *t'havir* (cf. eye), *teral liynikhar.*

Block, lump, clod, *khunv.*

Blood, *ziskhv, ziskh* (G. *siskhli*).

Blood feud, vendetta, *litsvri.*

Blow, stroke, *naqer* (G. *garda-nacari*).

Blue, *urzhi* (G. *lurdchi,* azure); sky-blue, *detsemp'herish,*
   det- sep'herish (cf. sky and colour).

Blueberry (see whortleberry).

Blunt., *luvre* (? G. *dalabra*).

Boar (wild), *uelurkham, varulkham, valyur* (cf. G. *veluri,* wild),
t'hakh, takh (G. takhi) (cf. pig).

Boast (to), *lip'hashtv;* he boasts, *ip'hashtuiel.*

Body, *tan, ten* (G. *tani*).

Bog. *dchib* (G. *dchaobi*).

Boil (to), *lidchab;* boiled, *mudchab.*

Boiler, kettle, *tskhuad.*

Bold, *mobqavi.*

Bolt, bar, *hurdum* (G. *urduli*).

Bone, *dchidchtsi, dchidchmi, dchudchu, dchidchv.*

Boole, *lair* (Lat.), *tzingi* (G. *tsigni*).

Boots, *chequmar, chekmaral* (G. *chekmebi*); footgear generally,
   byshkhem ledisk.

Borrow (to), *livleni* (cf. lend).

Bosom, lap, *kholezh.*

Both, *erquda, yerqyda.*

Bound, tied, *lotzirkhe, lutzkhansha.*

Boundary, *zghvid* (G. *zghude,* wail).

Bow (archery), *khemad.*

Box-tree *(Buxus sempervirens), sakal.*

Boy, *dchqint'h, bep'hsh* (G. *bavshvi*).

Bracelets, *kheshnauri.*

Brain, marrow, *t'hael, t'hvel* (G. *tvini*).

Bran, *gat, giad* (G. *kato*).

Branch, *arshkhal, ashkhal.*

Brass, *chei.*

Bravery, *lymarg, lymargv.*

Bread, *diar* (gen. sing. *diri*); bread for the priest after the liturgy, *tablash.*

Break (to), *liqvshe*; they broke, *akushekh.*

Breakfast, *ulup'h* (any meal), *khevsa* (morning meal).

Breast, *mudchod, mudchved, mudchvet'h.*

Breastplate, cuirass, abjar (G.); breastplate of a horse, *chap'hrid.* Bride, *lekhkhuri, letsvile.*

Bridegroom, *lechzheri, lechshori (lichizhe,* to marry).

Bridge, *bog* (G. *bogiri*).

Brilliant, *myklyne.*

Bring (to), *likhdekh, likhdune, li, lihhdc*; he brought, *kokhkud;* bring hither (sing.), *anikhd;* to bring up, rear (a child), *litskhmune.*

Broad, *masheri.*

Brother (of a sister), *dchimil,* pl. nom. *ladchmila,* pl. gen. *ladchmilre;* (of a brother), *mukhbe,* pi. *lakhuba, lakhna;* brother-in-law (wife's brother), *semun,* pl. *lasmuna;* brotherhood, *limkhub.*

Brow, *nep'hkui, nebgua, nagvba, nigba.*

Brush, *kuindchil.*

Brushwood, *kuadal.*

Buckle, *khardjik.*

Bud, *kuimpr.*

Builder, *myshnavi* (G. *sheneba*, to build).

Bull, *bughva*.

Bullet, *p'hunt'hukhv, p'hindukh, p'hindigh, tzkhvi* (G. *tqvia*). Bundle, *ladcher, k'hap*; to bind, *lidchreni*.

Burn (to), *lishkhi, zhilibdine*; it was burned down, *akhshikhena*. Bury (to), *lisht'hkhui, lishdkhvi, lishdghvi*; they buried,

    asht'hukhekh; burial, *chrashtukh*.

Business, *gvesh*.

But, *mare*; *mar, yago.*

Butt (of a gun), *dzur.*

Butter, *letzvmi* (? G. *chumi*).

Butterfly, *parpond* (cf. G. *pepela, p'harp'hara*, and Lat. *papilio*). Button, *legem, ghil*, pi. *p'holkar* (G. *p'holaki*).

Buy (to), *liqdi.*

C

Cake, pie, *kut'h, kubdar* (G. *cupati*): cake made of millet and

    cheese, *dchishv'thar.*

Calf, *ghun, ghunua.*

Calf of the leg, *pashvd, paasht.*

Call (to), summon, *lituli.*

Calm, *shvidbian* (G. *mshvidi*).

Campaign, expedition, *nalashgari* (cf. army). Candle, *letvre.*

Cannon, *jazail* (G.), *zarbazani* (G.).

Cap, hat, *p'haqv (papakh), luqundip'haqv* (of sheepskin).

Carbine, *qut'hkhva.*

Carefully, cautiously, *mckvbad.*

Caress (to), *lip'hrebal* (G. *p'hereba*).

Carpenter, *mutabe.*

Carpet, *nokh, nekhv* (G. *nokhi*).

Carry (to), *lighuane.*

Cat, *tsitsr* (G.). dim. *tsitsuld*; kitten, *kitav.*

Catarrh, cold in the head, *machkhuna.*

Catch (to), *lirmi*; he caught, *at'horma.*

Cattle, *kumash, vetkhmaval.*

Cave, *kvab* (G.).

Caw (to), croak, *liqulhune.*

Ceiling, *lydcher* (G. *dcheri*).

Cellar, *diuleg, gem.*

Certain one (a), *ierkhi* (G. *ert'hi*).

Chaff, *libale.*

Chain, *nadcha* (G.); chained, *lushkad* (cf. blacksmith).

Chair, *skam* (G.), *saskam.*

Chalice, cup, *bardzim* (cf. G. *Bardzimiani,* the Holy Grail, *bardzi,* blood of Christ, *bardzimi,* cup, chalice). Chamois, *yersken.*

Change (to), *litsadi.*

Charcoal, *shiikh* : live coal, *ghuerghad, ghvirch, ghyrch, mughvaz.*

Cheap, *iep'h* (G. *iep'hi).*

Cheat (to), *lighrovi.*

Cheek, *aqba, haqba.*

Cheese, *t'hesh, tash.*

Cherry, *heb, gaebe* (both fruit and tree).

Chest, box, *skivr* (G. *scivri).*

Chestnut (*Castaiica vesca), guidchi, gvidj, quich.*

Chicken, *tsitsil, tsintsil* (G. *tsitsila).*

Child, *bebshi, bebshv, bobsh* (G. *bavshvi), dchqint'h, pitsqil;* children, *bobshar;* childhood, *ligzel.* Chin, *niktza, nikare* (G. *nicapi).*

Chintz, *chimt'h* (G. *chit'hi).*

Choose, elect, prefer, *lilque, litskhane, zhililqvhc, lit'hsli;* chosen, elected, *nalqui;* choose (imp. sing.), *zhakhulkvih.*

Christ, *Kristes.*

Christening, *lepristi* (? cf. Christ).

Church, *mezra, lakuam, lakhvam, lakhumi.*

Churchyard, *sasp'hlav* (G. *sasap'hlao).*

Clay, *oqal* (G. *aqalo);* made of clay, *voqlar.*

Clean (to), *lishdbune, likvtzani.*

Clear (sky), *matzkhe.*

Clearly, in order, *lumskadad.*

Cleft, chink, crack, *p'hutu.*

Clever, *bazhian, chqvian* (G. *chqviani*).

Climb (to), *zhilizi.*

Cloak (of felt), *ghart'h.*

Cloth, *skalat* (G. *sclati,* Gr. *skarlatton*), *kuli.*

Clothing, *lercqv, lerkual.*

Cloud, *lamerua, mere, mare;* clouds, *marolar.*

Coat (of sheepskin), *keesh ;* overcoat, *uosare.*

Cock (bird), *qvech, quich, momal* (G. *mamali*).

Cock (of a gun), *chakhmakh* (G.).

Coffin, *kub* (G. *cubo*).

Cold, *mytskhi* (both subst. and adj.).

Colic, *khadmezgi* (cf. belly and disease).

Collect (to), *limaral, zhilindclvme, lizvri, lizvriale, lizvreni:* he

    collects, *inzaralal.*

Colour, *p'her* (G.), *ruhy, hab* (cf.

cherry). Colt, *sabel.*

Column, *sot* (G. *sveti*).

Comb, *latskhnir.*

Come (to), *liqed, lizi, linkhri, likhed;* I come, *uri;* they
    come, *agrikh;* they had come, *agrit'hakh;* come here!
    agher, come with me! *minkher;* to come in, *liched;* he
    came in, *chode.*

Command (to), *liqqani.*

Companion, comrade, *ap'hkhnek, amp'hkhni* (G.
amkhanagi),

    atzkhney, pl. *atzkhnegar;* travelling companion,
munkhri. Complain (to), *lichivle* (G. *vuchivi,* I complain).

Complexion, *heb* (cf. colour).

Condition, agreement, *pirob* (G.). Conquer (to), *zliilitznavit limtzir.*

Conscience, *namu* (G. *namusi*).

Consent, approval, *qeru.*

Contradict (to), *litskhide.*

Conversation, to converse, *ragiad, limgual, limbual* (G.).

Copper, *spilendj* (G.); made of copper, *cheish* (cf. brass); copper vessel, *t'hving.*

Copse, *jigir* (G. *jagnari*).

Corn, grain, *it'hq;*

corn-bin, *kibden* (G.), *kibduen.*

Corner, *kut'hkhv* (G. *cut'hkhe*).

Corpse, *dzver* (G. *mdzovri*).

Couch, *takht'h* (G. *takhti*).

Cough, *khvash* (G. *khvela*): to cough, *liqshiel.*

Count (to), *lishildani* (from *sheld,* number).

Country, land, *khev* (G. *khevi* - glen).

Court (to), beg, supplicate, *limkhal.*

Courtyard, yard, *qor.*

Cousin, *lakhbagezlir.*

Cow, *p'hyr, p'hyrv* (G. *p'huri*).

Cowardice, *limqal:* cowardly, *maqlyvar.*

Crack, crevice, *p'hut'hu.*

Cradle, *aquan* (G. *acvani*).

Crawl (to), creep, *libobal.*

Cream, *nagheb* (G. *naghebi*).

Croak (to), caw, *liqulhune.*

Cross, *dchvari* (G.); sign of the Cross, *starvin* (Gr. *stavros*).

Crust (of bread), *dzgid.*

Cry (a), shout, *kit* (cf. G. *cilo*, tune).

Crystal, *brol* (G.), *mintzora, mutzura* (? G. *mina*, glass).

Cuckoo, *giago* (G. *guguli*).

Cunning, trickery, *heriob*; adj. *hiria*.

Cup, *t'has* (G.), pl. *t'hasar, p'hakian*; large cup, *kob, bardzim*
  (cf. chalice).

Curd, *tot*.

Currant (bush, fruit), *muntskhar* (G. *motzkhari*).

Curse (to), *lichte, lidcht'hune, litsval*: may he curse, *ot'hdchat'huna*.

Cut (to), *litseni, litsqeni*; to cut off, *liqvtsure, lichkvre liqvtse*; he cut off, *kat'hkuits*; to cut down, *lidchgori*.

D

Dagger, *khandjar* (G.).

Damage (to), *mushurias.*

Dance (a), dchishkash lishpare; to dance, lisbi, lishushpari.

Darkness, *mubur, mubvir, libure*; to get dark, *libvre.*

Daughter, *dina,* dim. *dinol.*

Dawn, *ruhi* (cf. colour), *lirhal, iburghan*; to dawn, *lirhal.*

Day, *ladegh* (G. *dghe)*; in the daytime, *ladeghn*; to spend the
day, *lildeghi.*

Deacon, *dikven.*

Dead, *ludgar, lydgiar* (G. *mcvdari).*

Deaf, *qormandji, qurmedj, quk, qurman* ((J. *qru).*

Dear, expensive, *dzvir* (G.).

Death, *dagra, chvadgan.*

December, *Barblash.*

Deep, *skodi, nuchtzui*; depth, *naskodi.*

Deer, *lachv, liachv, iron* (G.).

Deformed, *kholalatsvash* (cf. bad).

Demon, *devi, djinn, dav* (G. *devi),*

Deserter, *namched.*

Desire, wish, *hadv, likved.*

Despise (to), *lisge.*

Devil, *eshmag, ashma* (G. *eshmaci), qadj, kanji* (Ar.), *hovm*
(cf. Jew), *mabeger.*

Dew, *tsuar* (G. *tzvari), rir, bibkh.*

Die (to), *lidgari, lidgiari*; he is dead, *chuadgan, chnadugan:*
dead, *ludgar.*

Difficult, *t'hemi.*

Dig (to), *liburdje.*

Diminish (to), *limyrkhelde.*

Dinner, *sadil* (G.), *ulup'h* (any
meal). Direct, straight (adv.),
metsvind. Direction, *namtsvin.*

Disappear (to), be lost, *lit'hphe*; he disappeared, *at'hunp'h.
at'huaph, nodchlekedi.*

Discover (to), find out (about something), *likvhe*; he
found out, *adkvih.*

Disease, *mazig, legmerde.*

Dish, *djar, gveb.*

Dislocation, luxation, *liqvech, ligeb.*

Displease (to), *lilone.*

Dissolute, dissipated, *bozai* (G. *bozi,* a whore).

Distant, *dchvedia.*

Ditch, trench, *t'hkhril (G. t'hkhrili).*

Divine, *ghert'ha* (cf. god).

Do (to), make, *lichem, lisht'hab*; do! (sing.), *khak*; to do
anything to anybody, *liqrine.*

Doctor, *akim* (G. *ekimi*).

Dog, *qurcha, zhigh, zhegh* (G. *dzaghli*); bitch, *dchua*; pup,
p'hakvna; kennel keeper, *mezhegh.*

Door, *kari* (G.), *qor, qorv.*

Dough, *khitz.*

Dove, *mukv, mugv.*

Down, *clukuan.*

Dowry, *nachvlash.*

Dragon, *greliarshap* (G. *gveleshapi*).

Drawers (of men), *arshule*; (of women), *zuralash arshuil*.

Dream, *isnau, istam*; to dream, *liistam, listam*; I dreamt, *lamistam*; he dreamt, *lakhistam*.

Drink (to), *litre, kit'hre* (cf. G. *vit'hvrebi* and *mt'hvrali*); drinking, *lat'hra*; drinking vessel, *lat'hra*; to drink up, *chulitre*: to get drunk, *chulishdme*.

Drop (of liquid), *tsvet'h* (G. *tsvet'hi*).

Drought, *gval* (G. *gvalva*).

Drowned (to be), *lishgodi*; you will be drowned! *esshgudand*. Drunk, intoxicated, *mashdmar*: drunkenness, *lishdume*.

Dry, *p'huri*.

Duck, *multz, milts, tsqashind*.

Dumb, *blu, bliv*

Dust, *birghv*.

Dyer, *mykhpörv* (G. *mghebari*).

E

Each, *mag, t'hvit'h* (G.), *t'huit'hzhin, chi, chie;* each other, *ushguare,   ushkhuar,*
ushkhvar. Eagle, *verb* (G. *orbi*).

Ear, *sht'hum₁ sht'henum, net'hunen, shtish, shtam, chimrale, shdim,* pl. *shdumar;* ear of corn, *shda.*

Early, *dosd.*

Ear-rings, *lcsht'hmarar, leshdmaral;* ear-ring, *leshdim.*

Earth, *gimas, gim, ver;* earthen, *voral.*

East, *lezh, lezhe, lezha; ;* eastern, *zhabe.*

Eat (to), *lizveb, lizob, chulidiaral (diar,* bread), *livlup'hal.*

Eclipse (of the sun), *betzelibure (? detselibure,* cf. heaven and
darkness), *mizhemlibure* (cf. sun); (of the moon), *doshdlali- bure* (cf. moon.).

Edge, *pil* (G. *piri,* mouth).

Egg, *ligre,* pi. *ligraal;* white of egg, *tsil* (G. *tzila);* yolk, *gvi* (cf. heart) ; egg-shell, *kian.*

Eight, *ara* (G. *rva).*

Elhow, *chit'hkh.*

Elbruz (Mount), *Yalbuz.*

Elm (*Ulmus campestris*), *stskymra.*

Embrasure of a tower, *shdul, shdur, santzkhvir.*

Emperor, *keser* (G.), *khentzipe* (G.).

Empty, *lerqene, tsariel* (G.).

Enclosure, fence, *dzghuidi* (cf. boundary).

End, *khem, pilu, pit* (cf. edge); to end, *ligt'havi* (G.); finally, *khomas, ghoshgunpils.*

Enemy, *amakhv.*

Enough, *masard, kali, bizli*; to be enough, *lire*; it was enough for him, *kut'hkhade* ; it will he enough for us, *qagnar.*

Enquire (to), *lidchvdiel.*

Entertain a guest (to), *likhnie* (cf. G. *Ikhini)* (cf. feast).

Environs, *zghudil* (cf. boundary and enclosure).

Eternally, *ivas.*

Evening, *nahoz*; in the evening, *nabos.*

Everywhere, *chiag* (cf. *chi*, each, all).

Ewe, *laila.*

Ewer (copper vessel like a coffee-pot), *['living* (G. *Vhunyi).*

Exchange (to), *litzadi.*

Excrement, fteces, *nasken.*

Exhaust (to), *lishtkhe.*

Eye, *t'he* (G. *t'hvali), let'he*, pl. *t'herar*; a man with eyes in his head, *lute*; to cast the evil eye, bewitch, *nat'hulquen*; pupil of the eye, *tsughvaz*; white of the eye, *как*; eyebrow, *nekdcha, nikhtsha,* eyelash, *t'halap'ha, t'halap'hal.*

F

Face, *vishkv, uishkv.*

Faith (religion), *dchruli (G. rdjuli).*

Falcon, *shevarden, shavarden (G.), mimil (?).*

Fall (to), *lishqed, lip'ieshvt;* he fell, kamchu, qamchu; they fell, *ashqadkh;* to fall down, ligvramal, ligruanal.

Famous, *lup'hiash, lahrak.*

Far, *dchodia, dcliodian, dchedia, dchvedia, djodiash, djuedias.*

Farewell (to bid), *lishdobal.*

Farmer, cultivator, *motskhne* (cf. to plough).

Fast (a), *markhv (G. markhva), lilchal;* to fast, *liudchmi.*

Fat (subst.), *chqan*   (G. *koni*), adj. *megre;* to grow fat, *likvashgi.*

Fatal, fateful, *leshti.*

Father, *mu (G. mama),* gen. sing. *muve,* nom. pl. *mular;* father-in-law, *mimt'hil (G. mamamt'hili);* stepfather, *muenatsad (G. maminatzvali);* grandfather, *baba.*

Fatigue, *lip'hash.*

Fear, *maqal.*

Feast, banquet, to feast, *lakhedal, lakhiadal (G. lkhini),*

Feathery, *shkhar.*

Feed (to), *lidiarne (diar,* bread).

Felt (material), *nahad (G.).*

Fence, *zghvid, dzghvid* (cf. boundary, enclosure, environs); to

fence in, *lidzghdi.*

Fern, *gymor (G. gvimra).*

Festival, *vikvm (G. ukmi)* (cf. holiday).

Fettered, chained, *lushkad* (cf. blacksmith and chain); to fetter,

liburkile: fetters, *berkliar* (G.

borcili). Fever, *mantzkhia, mait'hra.*

Fidelity, *lirt'hkul (G. ertguleba).*

Field, *mind or, mindver* (G. *mindori*); cornfield, *dab* (G.

daba,

village).

Fifty, *rokhvishdeshd.*

Fight (to), *lishal.*

Fill (to), *ligershli.*

Finally, *khomas, ashkhunechkhav.*

Find (to), *likhvie*; you found, *adjkhuid*; he found, *okhuida*;

to lind out, *zhilimkhare*; find out! (pl.), *zhakhmekhred.*

Finger, *t'hi* (G. *t'hit'hi*), *p'hkhule, phkhole*; finger-nail,

tzkharal, tzkharar.

Fir (*Abies orientali*), *ghumir, gumyr, maghra; (Abies Nord-*

manniana), *nense* (G. *nadzvi*).

Fire, *lemes, lemesy*; to light a lire, *lishve.*

First, *eshkhu, t'khuem, mankui* ; first of all (previously),

mankwi, chiq.

Fish, *qalmakh, calmakh* (G. *calmakhi*, trout); fishing-rod,

ankes

(G. *ancesi*).

Five, *volchvishd.*

Flea, *zysq* (G. *vtsqili*).

Flint (for striking fire), *kadch* (G.), *tol.*

Flock, herd, *dchueg*; flock of birds, *kharvan*

(caravan). Flood, *litzilitzkhem* (cf. water).

Floor, *lydchrave.*

Flour, *p'hek* (G. *p'hkvili*); flour-bin, *kibdven;* flour-mill, *legvher (ligweh*, to grind).

Flow (to): it was flowing swiftly, *ghuarsemizda.*

Flower, *dadil,* dim. *dadilud* (?); flowers, *mughuai.*

Fly, *meer* (G. *mtseri).*

Fly (to), *liper, liperiel,* (frequentative) *lipanal.*

Foam, *per* (G. *peri).*

Fodder, *lezveb* (cf. eat).

Fog, *dindgvil.*

Follow (to) (run after), *lidchem;* he is following me, *madchim.* Food, *luzub, lezveb* (cf. eat).

Fool, *dau.*

Foot, *dchiskh, dchish, dchisk, dchishekh, kishk;* on foot, *kveit'h* (G.); foot of a hill, *dzir* (G. *dziri,* root); footpath, *lakdaban.*

Forbid (to), *lidurvani.*

Ford, *ladt'hkhel, p'hion* (G. *p'honi).*

Forehead, *nebgva, nep'hkui, nigba.*

Foreign, *khevish* (cf. country); foreigner, *ishknemi.*

Forest, *tskheq, tskhek* (G. *tqe*); woody, *tskheqi.*

Forever, *ivas, chigarishd* (cf. all).

Forget (to), *chulishdne.*

Forgive (to), *lizhri, lishdobal.*

Fortress, castle, *muqwam.*

Fortune-telling, *lalobwal* (stone on which divination is practised):

to tell fortunes, *lilobwal.*

Forward, *sgebin.*

Foundation, *khun.*

Four, *vosht'h, voshdkhv.*

Fox, *mal* (G. *mela*).

Fracture, *likvesh.*

Fraud, *liyhroval* (cf. cheat).

Free, *t'havisnphal* (6.) (lit. lord of head or self); freedom, *lit'havisup'hle*; liberated, *lit'havisuphleli*; freely, *t'havisup'hald.*

Freeze (to), *likvremi* (cf. *kvarem*, ice); hoar-frost, *duser.*

Friday, *uebish, vebish, vobish, mebish.*

Friend, *tsal,* pl. *latsla, abkhneg* (G. *amkhanagi*), *hertz*; friendship, *mykt'ho'h.*

Frighten (to), *liqalve* (cf. fear, *maqal*).

Frog, *ap'hkhv, amp'hkhv* (G. *baqaqi*).

From, *ka.*

Front (in), *sguebin.*

Frost, *kvarem* (cf. freeze and ice); frozen, *lukvrame.* Froth, *per* (see foam).

Fruit, *khil* (G.); to bear fruit, *lislne*; mixed fruits, *khilmakhil.* Fugitive, deserter, *namchad.*

Full, gveshi, gueshi, groshi, goshi bingoshia, imgoshili, ingoshili;

fullness, *ligvshile.*

Funeral, *nashtghun, lashdkhval*; funeral feast, *lagvan.*

Fur cloak, *keesh* (cf. coat).

G

Game (hunting), *nat'huiare.*

Gamecock (? ptarmigan), *musur.*

Garden, *bagh* (G.); vegetable garden, *lart'ham* (G. *bostan*).

Garlic, *nivra* (G.).

Gate, *hazuaqor.*

Gentian *(Gentiana cruciata)*, *djager.*

Gentleman, *p'hust'h, lebsugh.*

George (St.), *Djurag, Djughurag, Dchguragi.*

Gift, *sachukar* (G.), *zhir, zhyr.*

Gild (to), *linkrovi* (cf. gold).

Gird (to), *lilortqe*; girdle, *lartq* (G. *sartqeli*).

Girl, *simaq.*

Give (to), *livde, likhvdi, lihvdi*; he gave, *ivomune, kaulamome*; give! sing. *lame,* pl. *lakhuemd*; let him give! *kovlakhuem;* I shall give, *qakhuavdi, qadchaudi*; give us, *qalano;* I shall give thee, *ladchodi*; he gave to him, *khahvedda.*

Glad (to be), *libazh, lichone*; he was glad, *at'humbazhun.*

Glass (material), *dchik* (G. *dchika)*; (tumbler), *kat'hkhul.*

Glitter, lustre, *muqure.*

Gloves, *kheshmar, khelt'hat'hmar* (G.).

Gnat, *kughnar.*

Go (to), *lizi, liqrab, lizhegh* (to go forward); I come, *ghuri*; I come hither, *enghuri*; he wᵉent, *khozhoghda, amched*; go there! *adgher* (sing.); go! (pl.) *oskhurid*; to go thither, *chulizi*; he goes, *esghuri, eskhri*; they are setting out, *esghurikh*; I shall go, *esghurine*; to go in

front, *lizhuegh*; he went in front, *emzhogh*; to go out,
kalizi (*ka*, from).

Goat, *dakhul, p'hikv, zurai*; wild goat, *yersken*; young
goat, *neghshti, neghasht*.

God, *ghertem, gherti, ghmerti* (G.), *ghermet, gherbed*.

Goitre, *quich*.

Gold, *okvr, vokr, vokvr* (G. *okro*); golden, *okvresh,
okvrcmish*.

Good, *khocha, dadil* (cf. flower), *ezalli, ezar, khochemi,
bednieri* (good-hearted, cf. G.); very good (used of
gold in fairy tales), *khalas*; good fellow, *bednier*.

Goose, *gkarghlad, gkarghad, bat* (G.).

Grain (cereals), *diar* (cf. bread), *kakal* (G. *cacale*, nut, grain).

Granary, *maran* (G.).

Grandfather, *baba*; grandmother, *dada, tata*; grandson,
nebashi, gezlash, gezal.

Granite, *gurna*.

Grapes, *qurzcn, qurdzcn* (G.).

Grass, *chqivar, balakh* (G.).

Grasshopper, *myntzla*.

Gratitude, *madil* (G.), *hasham*.

Gravel, *gub*.

Great, *dzkhod* (G. *didi*), *khosha*.

Green, *cirzhi* (cf. blue).

Grey, *parv*; greyish, *momprev, kvishemperish*; grey-haired,
khosgiar.

Grind (to), *ligweh*.

Groan (to), *likvetz*.

Group, *dehurti* (G. *jgupi*).

Grow up (to), *zkilitzkhem*; to grow, *litskhem*.

Guard (to), *liqrule* (G. *qaraul*).

Guest, *mushgua, mushgvri*; to be a guest, *limshgvar, limshgoral.*

Guide, *sguebin, muzhvegh.*

Guilty, *danashavir* (G. *damnashave, shavi* black).

Gun, *t'hep'h, t'hhop'h*; rifle, carbine, *qut'hkhva, kolaqut'hkh, kolaqut'hkhva*; gun-barrel, *stvir* (cf. Russ. *stvol)*; muzzle, *khuru*; flint, *tol(G.)* (see also cock, butt, ramrod, powder, etc.).

H

Habit, custom, *limt'hkve*.

Hail, *skarkhal*; to hail, *liskurkhali*.

Hair, *p'hat'hv*, pl. *phat'hvar, lust'hgu*; plait, tress, braid of hair, *lusdigv*.

Halter, *hap'hshara* (G. *avshara*).

Ham, *lerv, lor* (G. *lori*).

Hammer, *tzurol, tzirol* (G. *tserakvi*), *qwaba, qveba, kuat'hkh, quer* (G. *cveri*).

Hand, *shi*, pl. *shiar, shun, t'hot'h, t'hot'hil, tvet*, gen. sing, *toti*, pl. nom. totar; right hand, *mursghven t'hvet'h*; left hand, *mirt'hen t'hvet'h*; nails, *tzkharal*; fingers, *p'hkhuliar*; palm, *mimi guigv*.

Handkerchief, *lep'hkhvnashy lakvtzan*.

Hang, intr. *lirkune*, tr. *liqme*.

Happen (to), *liqrine*; it happened, *dcheqar, khochinda*.

Happy, *lukchev*; happiness, *libednier* (G. *bednieroba*).

Hard, *bygi, bygiar* (G. *magari*).

Hare, *rack, rachv*, dim. *rachuld*.

Harrow, *ladchadir, ber*.

Harvest, *mosawal* (G.); to harvest, *lit'hi*.

Hat, *p'hsaku* (cf. cap).

Hate (to), *lissge*; hatred, *orgulob* (G.).

Have (to), *lighvane;* I have, *mam, mar*; I have (an inanimate object), *mighva, mughwe, mughwa*; thou hast, *djigva, djiri*; thou hast much money, *si djiri khvai t'het'hr*; I had, *mighvanda*; thou hadst, *djighvanda, dchughvan*; he had, *qonda* (G.); I havo a horse, *khad maqa chazh;* I havo money, *mughw t'het'hr*.

Hawk, *tzkhakv.*

Hay, *chem;* hay meadow, *lare.*

Hazel *(Corylus avellana), shtukhund* (cf. nut).

He, *adcha, adja, edji.*

Head, *tlikhnm, tkhvish, t'hkhvim;* from head to foot, *t'hkhume dchislikhe;* on the head, *t'hkhumishi;* big-headed, *ashvorblian;* headlong, *ut'hkmul;* occiput, *lakhmir;* skull, *t'hkhvimihaqar;* crown of the head, *lat'hat'hiel;* temple, *laghadchir;* headache, *thkhumi mazig* (cf. disease), *t'hkhumish mazig.*

Health, *lishduebi, khochamdari.*

Heap, *dchurti* (cf. group and herd).

Heart, *gvi, gui, gu* (G.); I wish, *gvimar* (war, I have).

Hearth, *kera, kerai* (G.).

Heat, *at'hu.*

Heaven, *dets* (G. *zetsa).*

Heavy, *t'hymi, gvami* (G. *mdzime).*

Heel, *hagva, haguar.*

Height, *didab* (G. *dideba), naklat'hkhi.*

Heir, *emsede* (?Pers.).

Hell, *jochkhect'h* (G. *jojokhet'hi,* ?cf. *jojo,* lizard).

Hellebore *(Helleborus orientalis), karsin* (G. *kharis dzira).* Helmet, *azrunchi, zuirch.*

Help (to), *lished, litse, limurdjvi;* help! (pl.), *loguesht'sh;* let him help, *eshulogshcda, culogsheda, adchgulogsheda;* helpful, *nad.*

Hemp, (G. *canaphi,* cf. Lat. *cannabis);* hemp-seed, *gimbash.*

Hen, *kat'hal* (G.).

Hence, *amkhenchu, amkhanqa, amkhan.*

Hord, flock, *dchueg* (G. *djogi*).

Here, amech, *amcchu, ame*; down here, *amechu*; local, *amechunash*. Hero, *dchabigvi* (G. *chabuki*).

Hide (to), *lishkhvni, lipezh* (G. *p'hareba*).

High, *kylt'hi, kiitkhi, koltkhe*; higher, *khosha, kiitkhi*; highest, *gun kiithi*

Hill, *zug* (cf. place-name *Zugdidi*).

Him, *misi*; himself, *edj, edja* (in Lower Svanetia), *adj, adja* (in Ushgul); his, *mihia*.

Hither, *iska, amkhav, adjkhav, amkhal*. Hitherto, *at'hkhadv*.

Hive, *laghob* (G. *rogo*).

Hoar-frost, *duser*.

Hold *(to)*, *liqdani*; hold! (sing.) *lekhqeden*; I held, *mi miqdanan*; thou heldest, *si dchiqdanan*; he held, *acas khoqdanan*.

Hole, gap, rent, *latsigv, khuru* (G. *khvreli*).

Holiday, *viqvm* (G. *ukmi*), *lisgvresh* (cf. festival).

Holly *(Cratagus)*, *santsi*.

Holy, *tzkilian*.

Home, *argi*; homewards, *korvad* (cf. house).

Honesty, *namyrtali*.

Honey, *saradj, t'hvi*.

Honourable, *patiosani* (G.).

Hoof, *chilk* (G. *chliki, jlici*), *p'hol*.

Hook, *ghilk* (G. *khrici*).

Hoop (for casks), *betq*.

Hope (subst.), *imed* (G.); to hope, *limedi*.

Horn, *mudchu midchv, karakhs* (G. *rka*).

Horse, *chazh, chash, daidj* (G. Tatar *taidji);* bay horse *mytzram;* piebald, dappled horse, *amlak;* flying horse (in fairy tales), *rash* (G.); horse with white spot on forehead, *saghari chash;* stallion, *kuaril, qwaryul;* unbroken horse, *lenchq;* mare, *dchag;* mounted, equestrian, *lalsgura* (from *lisgvre,* to sit); foal, *sabol, sabel;* ambler, *t'hukvrig* (G.); on horseback, *mychazhi;* to mount a horse, *chazh liskvre;* to dismount, *cliazhi likekh;* to saddle, *lihingre;* to unsaddle, *hingirliked;* to shoe, *lishkadi;* horseshoe, *nashkadun;* belly-band, *musurtan;* horse-tail, *haquad, hauquet.*

Hostage, *dzeval* (G. *mzevali).*

Hot, *at'hu, athvi* (cf. heat).

Hour, *sat'h, saat'h* (G.); half an hour, *saat'hiygynsga.*

House, *agi, kor, qor;* uninhabited house, *uktsire, ukvtsir* (G. *okheri)* ; little house, *kuruld;* lower story, *machula;* upper story, *darbaz.*

How, *imzhi;* how much, *uoshia, isava.*

Howl (to), *litskuli.*

Hundred, *ashir* (G. *asi).*

Hunger, *maid;* hungry, *maidar;* to be hungry, *libune.*

Hunt (to), *lit'hkhvar;* hunting-ground, *lat'hlchuer;* hunting, chase, *lat'h, khuial, lat'hkhuiar;* hunter, *met'hkhvar, met'hkhviar, met'hkhvcri.*

Husband, *dchash, dchashmi;* future husband, *lechshori.*

Hut, *sadgem* (G. *sadgomi), karavi* (G. *caravi)* (cf. abode).

I

I, *mi* (G. *me*).

Ice, *ol, uol, hol, kuarem.*

Iconostasis, *samkar* (? G. *sami*, three, and *cari*, door).

If, *ckhiy ere, he, hessa.*

Ill, sick, *legmerde*; to be ill, *lizge* (cf. disease).

Image, icon, *khat'h* (G.).

Immediately, *shislid.*

In, *ska* (suffix).

Incense, *sakmel* (G. *sacmeli*).

Indecent (to be), *lishgde.*

Inexhaustible, *usht'hikha.*

Inform (to), *likmari, libzhine.*

Ink, *melan* (Gr., G.).

Inside, *iska, ska, isgan, isga, isganchu.*

Instead, *muqajsh.*

Interpreter, *monin* (cf. tongue).

Interrupt (to), *lizhme.*

Into, through, *lisga.*

Invite (to), *litsse, litznavi.*

Iron, *beredj, berezh*; made of iron, *herzhcmisli, herzhash*; made
of cast iron, *chvhenura*; of wrought iron,
lyshkiad. Itch, *makhera* (G. *mghieri*).

J

January, *Kuagh, Kvakh.*

Jar (large), *kets*; jar, *stama, staman* (a liquid measure).

Jesus Christ, *Eshu Kriste, Kristesua.*

Jew, *viria* (G. *uriai*) *uriiai.*

Joke (to), *lilgatsal, likhvmaral.*

Journey, *gzavroh* (G.); to start on a journey, *lingzavre.*

Joy, *sarvoshale, khiad, lekhiad* (G.), *likhiriul* (G. *sikharuli*);

    joyful, *makharobel* (G. *mkhiaridi*), *lykhiadal* (G. *lkhini*)

Jump (to), *lisknal;* to jump out, up, *lisqne*; he jumped up,
    okhosquna; he jumped over, *kaisqine.*

Juniper (*Juniperus* sp.), *dchkeru.*

Just, right, *mart'hal* (G.).

K

Keg, *vokhar.*

Kettle, *tskhuad, tzkhvadv.*

Key, *kel, kyl* (G. *clite,* cf. Pers. and Lat.).

Kick, *ishvd.*

Kill (to), *lidgari* (cf. die, death); he killed, *adgar, adghar, chukhodgara*; they killed, *chadgarkh, chuadgarkh.*

Kind, sort, *rigi* (G.).

Kindle (to), light a lire, *lishve.*

King, *kheltziph* (G. *khelmtzip'he*).

Kinsman, *tzam.*

Kiss, *kalemqaen*; to kiss, *likhhaal.*

Knee, *ghula, gulai, kutulai, hulaika, ghualait'hkhwn, chveg*; he knelt, *cheschoqve*; knee-breeches, *zedkhar.* Knife, *giadj.*

Knock, *byrgyn.*

Know (to), *likhal, litzukh*; not to know, *madma likhal*; I know, *mitzokh, chumit'hra*; you knew, *dchikhaldakh*; not knowing, *ukhla.*

L

Ladder, *kichkh.*

Lady, princess, *luph'kel.*

Lake, *myh, tob* (G. *tba*)

Lamb, *zhinagh, zhingh*; to lamb, *lizhneghi.*

Lame, *chort'ha, kvachkhai, mykli.*

Lance, spear, *shub* (G.).

Land, *ver*; plot of land, *adgil* (G.).

Landslide, *zheh.*

Large, *khosha, dzghid* (G. *didi*).

Lasso, *balir.*

Late, to be late, *lirage.*

Laugh (to), *litsnal, litsvnal, litzunal* (G.); laughter, *latsu* (G. *sitzili*).

Laurel (*Daphne glomerata*), *madjora.*

Lazy (to be), *limchire, limchirval*; lazy, *mamdjirval*; laziness, *limchir.*

Lead, *tqve, tkhö* (G. *tqvia*); leaden, *tqvemish.*

Lead (to), *li*; he led, *esqa.*

Leaf, *bale.*

Leather, *t'hup'h, gwuäre.*

Left (hand), *lart'hen* (G. *martzkhena*); when of the 1st per., *murten.*

Leg, thigh, *makudshage.*

Lend (to), *livleni* (cf. borrow).

Length, *nadchvdi.*

Lentils, *kirs, kirtzi.*

Leprous, scabby, *khuarsa.*

Lie (to), lay, *liqvre, lide*; he lies, *khas*; he lay, *khadena*; lying, *meqvre*.

Life, to live, *lirde* ; I live, *khviri*; thou livest, *khiri*; he lives, *iri*; living, *merde, luvar*.

Light (not heavy), *hashi*.

Light, daylight, *ryhi*.

Lightning, *megh, mekh* (G. *mekhi*, cf. Arab, and Ann.), *lihlal*.

Like, alike, *khadjesh, madjona, khal*; like him, *khal adcha, adchzhi mi*

Like (to be), resemble, *lip'hesh*.

Linen, *sgvir, skyr* (G. *shira*).

Lip, *pil*; lips, mouth, *pilar* (G. *piri*).

Listen (to), overhear, spy, *livnari, lifnari, lihnari*; I listen, *khovnari*;   listen!   (sing.),

lokhhunar. Litter, stretcher, *chat'hr*.

Little, *kotol*.

Live (to), *lizge*; he lived, *khilzigal*; living, alive, *lyiar*.

Liver, *qvizhe* (G. *ghvidzli*).

Lizard, *hasht'hakv*.

Load, baggage, *barg* (G.).

Load a gun (to), *lisqe, linqene*.

Loan, *limpshten*.

Lock of a door, *kyliar* (cf. key).

Long, *djodi*.

Look (to), *lisgdi, isgdi, zhilitsvane*; he looks, *kot'hdzgi*; look! (pl.), *kaiakhsgiddal, zhakhtsvannd*.

Lord, God, *p'hust*.

Lose (to), *likravi*.

Louse, (G. *tili*).

Lousewort *(Pedicularis atropurpurca*, Nord.), *menkel*.

Love, *lilat*; to love, lilat; O beloved Christ! *ai lilo Qriste*; thou lovedst, *dchaltan*.

Low, *lekva* (G. *kvena*); lower, *chube, dzurmu*.

Lung, *perskvda* (G. *philtvi, phirtvi*).

M

Madder (*Rubia tinctoria*), *handra* (G.) (cf. azalea), (Mingr. *endro*).

Magpie, *khavich*.

Maize, *simind* (G.), *simidi*; maize straw, *chala* (G.).

Make (to), do, *lichem, lisgem, lisht'hab, lichume, lisqi*; they made, *achminkh, okhsqekh*.

Man, *mare* (homo), *amsuald, gvajmare* (vir); little man, *marol*; manliness, *limar*.

Mane, *p'hap'hal* (G. *p'hap'hari*).

Manger, *gval*.

Maple (*Acer campestre*), *pychvra*.

Mare, *chag*, pl. *chagar*.

Mark, sign, *nishani* (G.).

Marriage, *nishnoga* (cf. *nishani*, mark).

Marry a wife (to), *licit izhal, lachizltal, lichizhe*; he *married, iqi, kavachize*; to perform the wedding ceremony, *ligurgune* (cf. G. *gvirgvini*, crown); unmarried man, u*chizha*; married man, *lykhekhv*; man who wishes to marry, *mechizhal*; not every man can marry, *liaklival chi mad khobits*.

Marry a husband (to), *litzvile, litzvilal*; married woman, *qalatzuile*: unmarried woman, *utzvila*.

Marsh, bog, *dchib, chuib* (G. *dchaobi*).

Marten, *qwen* (G. *cverna*).

Mary (St.), *Lamaria, Lamria*.

Mass (to celebrate), *litbuli*.

Master, lord, *p'husd, p'hust'h*.

Mead (liquor), *rang* (G. *raki*).

Meadow, *ladchma.*

Meal (breakfast, dinner), *ulup'h* ; slight meal, *khevs.*

Measure, *lazma* (G. *zoma*); to measure, *lizme* (G. *zomiereba*).

Mediator, *metzkhuil, motzkul* (G. *motzikuli,* envoy, apostle).

Medicine, *zhagar, zhagiar;* medicine man, *melt'her, qad.*

Medium, central, *nesga, manesgure.*

Meet (to), *limkhvi, likhvie;* meet us! (sing.), *enkhvid;* to go to meet, *lizzvi.*

Meeting (of people), *lakhor.*

Melon, *nesvi* (G.); water-melon, *harpuzak.*

Melt (to), thaw, *lipzhune.*

Mention (to), *lirslvni.*

Merchant, *ghvadchar* (G. *vadjari*).

Merciful, *maldian* (G. *madliani*).

Mercy, blessing, *lamzur.*

Merry, *khyrul* (G. *mkhiaruli*); merriment, *khin* (G. *lkhini*); to be merry, *lilkhne* (G. *lkhinoba*).

Michael Archangel, *Mukem T'haringzel.*

Midnight, *isglet'h* (cf. night).

Milk, *ludjo, ludje* (G. *rdze*); sour milk, *martsven* (G. *matsoni);* to milk, *gali;* milker (masc.), *mushgi.*

Mill, *lekveer* (G. *tsiskvili*); millstone, *shira.*

Millet, *p'hatv, pötu, pötv* (G. *p'hcetvi*).

Mind, wit, *t'hvel, vhwel;* intelligent, *vlwclian.*

Mingrelia, *Zane;* Mingrelian, *Luznu;* native of Mingrelia, *Muzan.*

Miracle, *sakvrnl* (G. *sakvirveli*).

Mirror, *sark* (G. *sarce*) (cf. lluss. *zerkalo);* to look in the glass, *lisurkal.*

Miserly, *tsinguil.*

Misfortune, *dchir* (G. *djiri*, plague), *ubdorob* (G. *ubeduroba*); to become poor, *lidchir.*

Mist, *dindgvil, bintv, nisl* (G. *nisli*).

Mistake (to make a), *liqed, likiad;* you have made a mistake, *adjqat'hkh.*

Mistress (loman), *lelat.*

Mix (to), *lichdune, lichdine.*

Moisture, *myzhir.*

Monday, *Dashtish, Doshlish, Ducshdish, Dislidish, Unshdish* (cf. moon).

Money, *t'het'hr* (G.) ; *varchkhil* (G. *vertzkhli*, silver).

Monk, *ber* (G.).

Month, *dosht'hul, makhe, t'hev* (G. *tht'hve*), pl. *t'hevar.*

Moon, *dosht'hul, doshdul;* moonrise, *doshdlalakhad;* eclipse of the moon, *doshdlalibure;* full moon, *gveshi doshdul;* new moon, *mokhe doshdul* (cf. young).

Morning, *gham, ham, dziner, dzinar* (G. *dila*), *dzunar, dzurva;* in the morning, *ghamias, hams.*

Moss, *khavis* (G. *khavsvi*).

Mother, *ti, did* (G. *deda*), *dia, di* (in caressing form, *dede, diulu*).

Mother-in-law, *dimt'hil* (G. *dedamt'hili*),

Mountain, *t'hhang, zagar, t'hanagh,* pl. *t'hanyhar;* to cross a mountain, *lit'hnaghi;* mountainous, *t'hanghiash;* mountain chain, *zaghar, zagiar;* mountain top, *t'hanyha-kunchil;* mountain foot, *t'hanyhadzir* (G. *dziri,* root).

Mourn for (to), *lagunan.*

Mouse, *shdug.*

Moustache, *ulmash, urmash, ulmashar* (G. *ulvashi*).

Mouth, *kharkh, lakra, uishkv, pilar* (lips); gums, *viriaial.*

Move (to), *likhqvtunal, likt'hune*; he moved (himself), *et'hkut'hhan*; we moved, *kat'hkut'hand*; they moved, *kalai kut'hakh.*

Mow (to), reap, *liti, lichme*; mower (fern.), *mtashi.*

Much, *khvas, khvai, khuai, masard, vobash, obash*; as much, *mazu, osha.*

Mud, *talakh* (G.); muddy, *talkhaar.*

Multiply (to), *lip'hshire.*

Mushroom (edible), *tkobut.*

Music, *lashmar.*

Musket, *qurmil, t'hop'ha* (G. *t'hop'h*).

Mutton, *uiliakiashleghv* (cf. sheep and meat).

Muzzle, bore, *nichlehva.*

My, *mishgu, myshgvi, misliku, mishkui, mishgua*, pl. *nishgvei.*

N

Nail (of iron), *dchkuaral, musmar, lusmar, lurtsman* (G.).

Naked, bare, *metqop'he, metqvp'he, ghverkle.*

Name, *zhakhe* (G. *sakheli*).

Narrow, *nakhutsi.*

Nastiness, *veb.*

Nausea, *khola guimiz* (cf. bad, heart, and disease).

Navel, *chip* (G. *djipi*), *shtikhv.*

Near, *p'hedia, p'hedi, p'hedias.*

Necessary, *khaku, chukhaku*; he needs bread, *achas khaku diar*; for marriage a good man is necessary, *liakhvals khocha mare khaku.*

Neck (throat), *qia, qea* (G. *qeli*), *qinchkh, kinsh* (nape of neck) (G. *cintsi*); necklace, *lebar, dzivar* (cf. beads).

Needle, *nesqal* (G. *nemsi*), *nöfske.*

Neigh (to), *lichirkhine* (G.), *lit'hyrtyne.*

Neighbour, *mezbel* (G. *mezobeli*).

Nephew, *nibashin, nebashi* (cf. grandson).

Nest, *sabdar* (G. *sabudari*).

Net, *dchachui* (G. *dchadjvi,*).

Nettle, *mercel* (Mingr. *dchudchele*).

Nevertheless, *eshi.*

New, *makhe* (cf. young).

News, *ambav, ambau* (G. *ambavi*).

Night, *let'h*; midnight, *isgletäh*; to-night, *bazi*; in the night, *laat'hshv.*

Nine, *chkhara* (G. *tzkhra*).

No, not, *dessa, madma, nom, num, deme, dem, dom, desh, demis, mad, made, madeo, madu, mama*; do not, *num* as prefix with imperative; do not do that (sing.), *nom khich alas.*

Nobleman, *varg* (G. *vargi,* worthy).

Nobody, *daar, der.*

Noise, *tqbip'h.*

Noon, *isgladegh* (cf. day and midnight).

Nose, *nafkhvna, löpkhna, nepkhuna*; nostrils, *neshtral.*

Nothing, *madma, mama.*

November, *Sasish.*

Now, *at'hkhe* (G. *ekhla ats*).

Nowhere, *deme, demeghmu*; no whither, *demt'he.*

Number, *sheld*; 1, *eshku*; first, *mankvy*; 2, iori, *heri, iervi;* second, *merve;* 3, *semi*; third, *mesme*; 4, *voshtkhv*; fourth, *mesht'hkhve;* 5, *vokhvishd*; fifth, *mekhvshde;* G, *usgva, usgvashd*; 7, *ishgvid*; 8, *ara*; 9, *chkhara*; 10, *ieshd*; 11, *ieshd* eshku; 12, *ieshd iori*; 20, *ierveshd*; 21, *ierveshdi eshkhu;* 30, *semeshd (samveshd, ervesht'hi, esht'h)*; 40, *voshtkhveshd (urinervesht'hi)*; 50, *vokhvishdeshd*; 60, *usgvashd;* 70, *ishgudaashd*; 80, *araashd*; 90, *chkharashd*; 100, *ashir;* 101, *ashir eshkhu;* 200, *ioriashir*; 300, *semashir*; 1,000, *at'has*; 10,000, *iesht'hat'has.*

Nurse (wet), *dzidzai* (G. *dzidza).*

Nut, *sht'hekhi, shtukhund, shdikh, gak* (cf. hazel).

O

Oak, *dchihra, djïgra.*

Oath (to take an), *lymbanal*

Oats, *zint'hkh, suntkho, magdenar.*

Obedient, *muhnari.*

Offended (to be), *lisdike*; they were offended, *at'hsastkunkh.*

Offering (an), *namzurun.*

Often, *khvai* (cf. much).

Old, *mechi, djunel*: older, *mashen, makhvshib*; old age, *limachv*; old man, *mechi*; old woman, *mechi zural;* to grow old, *limche*; elected village elder, *makhvshi.*

On, *zhi* (suffix).

One, *eshkhu, ieshkhu, esho, eshu, eshkhvi*; one at a time, t'huit'hi (G.)

Onion, *khakhv* (G.).

Only, *gar, alagiar.*

Open (to), *likre*; open! (pi.), *kared, miqared;* they opened *miqarekh*; wide open, *mukar.*

Opinion (hope), *imed* (G.).

Or, *ed.*

Osset (an), *musvi, saval, musav*; ossetian, *savash, saviash, lusu.* Other, another, *merba, merme, ishgen.*

Our, *gvyshgvei, gvishkve, gvishge.*

Out, outside, *qa*; from the outside, *kamen*; out of doors, *qam*

Ox, *khan* (G. *khari), qan*; an ox that has never been yoked, *uskhrai*; an ox with a white spot on the forehead, *shkharil.*

P

Pace, step, *brakh*; between the legs, *nabrakhs*.

Pail, *gab, segda*.

Pair, *tqub* (G. *tqubi*).

Palm, span, *kamin*.

Pan (frying), *tap'hai* (G. *tap'ha, tap'haci*).

Paper, *kalghard* (G. *kaghaldi*).

Paradise, *samet'hkhv* (G. *samothkhe*).

Part, portion, *nat'hi, naqvil* (G. *natsili*).

Part (to), separate, *liqvle*.

Pass, defile, gorge, *t'huip'h, t'huibi, t'hubi, t'huba, t'huber, twib*

(dat. *tubas*), *tvib* (G. *kheoba*).

Pasture, *bavar*: mountain pasture, *lakhoard, lakhv*; hayfield, *lare*.

Path, *lakdaban, qashan*.

Patient, *mot'hmine* (G. *motmineba*).

Peace, *lisal*.

Peach, *atam* (G.).

Peacock, *p'harshmagi* (G. *parshavangi*).

Pear, *itzkh, bytsikh, ystz*.

Pearl, *marglit, margli, margali* (G. and Pers.).

Pearls (string of), on woman's costume, *grekhel*.

Peas, *gheder, ghedar, netsing geder* (cf. small and beans).

Pebble, gravel, *gub*.

Pen, *kalam* (G.).

Penis, *qom* (G. *qle*).

People, *khalkh* (G.).

Perhaps, *igebs, igabe*.

Permit (to), *likhvie*; permit me! (sing.) *khakhvi*.

Pheasant, *dakhokhu, khokhueb* (G. *khokhobi*).

Pig, *khom, kham, takh*; sow, *nezv* (G. *nezvi*); sucking-pig, *guech* (G. *gochi*).

Pigeon, *mukv, mugv*.

Pillow, *balish* (G.).

Pine-tree (*Pinus silvestris*), *ghugib, gogib*.

Pipe (for tobacco), *lat'hral* (cf. drink and smoke).

Pistol, *tanbacha* (G. *dambacha*), *laghlatar*.

Pitchfork, *p'hitsal* (G. *p'hutzkhi*).

Pity, *mazhur*; to pity, *litklabe*.

Place (room, quarters, abode), *larda, mukab*; place (generally), *adgil* (G.).

Place (to), put, *lidisg, lidi, ligem*; I place, *masda*; thou placest, *djasda*; he places, *khasda*; he placed, *esust'ha, adge* (G.), *umast'handa*.

Plague, *zham* (G. *zhami*).

Plane (to), *litabe*.

Plank, *p'hitzar* (G. *p'hitzari*).

Plate, *sain* (G.)

Play (to), *lighral, lishtlraal*.

Pleasant, *sasiamun* (G. *sasiamovno*).

Pledge, bet, wager, *dzewel* (G. *nadzlevi*).

Plough, *ghantsvish, gentzish*; to plough, *likhni* ; ploughing-time, *likhniel* (G. *vhkhnav*, I plough).

Plum, *kliau* (G. *kliavi*), *barqen*.

Pocket, *jib* (G. *jibe*).

Poisonous, *kharal, shkhamian* (G.) *shkhamar*; to poison, *lizhgeni*.

Poor, *dchirar*; to become poor, *lidchir* (G.), *lighnibe*; poor
man, *gharib* (G.).

Poplar *(Populus tremula)*, *iekhura*.

Porter, bearer, *mukap'hi* (G. *merikipe*).

Pot, *tunu* (G. *kotani*).

Potato, *kartofil*.

Pound (lb.), *(girvanqa* (G.).

Pour (to) out, *ligvshe*; pour out! (sing.), *khagvshas*.

Powder, *zhag, dchage*; powder-horn, *vaznai*.

Power, strength, *khamshash*; powerful, *lokmash*.

Praise, *zhakhe* (c-f. name); praiseworthy, *latakh*; to praise,
lip'hashdv, lip'hshvdi.

Pray (to), *limyjri, linzuri, likhural*; prayer, *lotz* (G.).

Precipice, *bghuith, nadzgvib*.

Prepare (to), *limare*; prepare! (pi.) *lamarad*.

Present, gift, *sachukar* (G.).

Press (to), crush, oppress, *linqli*.

Price, *p'has* (G.).

Priest, *bap, pap*.

Prince, *varg* (cf. G. to be worthy), *t'haud*, (G. *t'havad*).

Princess, lady, *lu'phkel*; princess in fairy tales, *nanul*.

Prisoner, *tqve* (G.), gen. *tqvemi*; to take prisoner, *lirmi*.

Probably, *gheurd, heurd*.

Promise, *lip'htze* (cf. G. *phitzi*, oath).

Property, *lemghveni*.

Provisions, *lezia*.

Prudence, *lynt'hkhal*.

Pudendum muliebre, *budum* (cf. *p'hutu*, G. *muteli* and
Lat.). Pumpkin, *kuakhne*.

Punishment, *sasjel* (G.); to punish, *lisyrjeli*.

Pup, *p'hakvna*.

Pupil, *let'hvri* (cf. teacher).

Pure, *tsqilian*; purest, *matsquliane*; Holy Ghost, *Tsqilian Qvin*
    (cf. soul). Purse, *djurdan*.

Pursue (to), follow, run after, *lighvech, lidchem*.

Put (to), *lidisg, lidesgi, lidi, ligem, likche, zhiligem* (cf. to place);
    put! (sing.), e*skach, zhatag*, to put on, *laide, likvem*.

Q

Quail, *shqazh, shqazhv.*
Quarrel, *lashal, qarqash, litzual*; to quarrel, *lishal.*
Queen, *dedp'hal* (G.).
Quickly, *chqard* (G. *chqara*).
Quiet, *tsqnar* (G.).
Quite, *mchad.*
Quoth he, *eser, roqv, uv, u, v* (cf. affixed G. o).

R

Rain, *wuchkha, uchkha.*

Rainbow, *detzdiarlq* (cf. heaven and girdle).

Raise up (to), *likche*; he raised, *ankache, akhkachin.*

Rake, *lishdik, lap'htzkhir* (G. *potzkhi*).

Ramrod, *chkhir.*

Ransom, *sakhsar.*

Rare, *dut'hkhel*; rarity, *dzvird* (G.).

Raspberry, *ingha, vykh.*

Rat, *madshidai.*

Raven, *ghvemal, dehwer* (? crow).

Raw (beef), *ziskhi* (cf. blood).

Razor, *tzabv, tsab.*

Read (to), *lichvdi*; he read, *tzevikitkha* (G.).

Ready, *lumarad.*

Real, *dadil* (G.) (cf. flower and good).

Reap (to), mow, *liti* (cf. mow); mower (masc.), *myt'hi.*

Recognize (to) (a person), *liter.*

Red, *tzine* (G. *tsit'heli*), *tzunu, tzurni, tzurnu, tsorny.*

Refusal, *var.*

Rejoice (to), *lichvne, likhiadal.*

Related, akin, *tsam.*

Remain (to), *lised*; he remained, *amsad, asad*; they remained, *amsadkh.*

Remember (to), *zhilishqed, lishqad*; he remembered, *zhilakhshqad.*

Repent (to), *lihdyre.*

Reproach, *mandrev* (G. *tsaqvedreba*).

Request (a), *shgom, likhyral.*

Resemble (to), *lidchem*; he resembles him, *khadchish*; thou
resemblest me, *si madchish*.

Respect (to), *likitzkhav, lishgural*.

Rest (to), *lishen, lishvem, lishuem*; unresting, *vismeqali*.

Return (to), come back, *litekh, goshlitekh, limekh*; they
returned, *osht'hat'hakh, vont'hakh*; he has returned,
lakhtakh.

Revile (to), *litsral*.

Rhododendron Caucasicum, *skore* (Imer., Mingr., and
Gurian,
shkeri, ? R. Ponticiim).

Rib, *kip* (G. *tsibo*, cf. thread); ribs, *lesg* (cf. side).

Rich man, *didar* (G. *mdidari*); to become rich, *liddari*.

Ridicule, *litzv*; ridiculous, *latzmar* (G. *satzinari)i*.

Riile, *qut'hkhva*.

Right hand (cf. hand), *lersgven, lesgvan*; when of the 1st
pers.,
mursgven; on the right, *lerskuankhen, lersgnamkhen*.

Ring, *muskad, myskiad* (cf. blacksmith, wrought iron,
horseshoe, chained, fettered).

Ringworm, *mykhchyl, lekhchi*.

Ripe, *muhi*.

Rise (to), get up, *lignal*.

River, *lits, dcliala, dclialaishu* (cf. water); rivulet, *litsuld,
tsqaro*
(G.), *sarak, tuibra, ?sargel*.

Road, *shuq, shuqa, shugv, shuk, shukv*, gen. *shukwi*, pl.
nom. *shukwar*; to make a road in the snow, *lichabi*; to
make a road, *lishkwi*.

Rob (to), *lighlati* (cf. G. *ghalati*, treachery).

Rock, *kodj, qodja.*

Roof, *lyqaar, lasg.*

Root, *becliashuam, dzir* (G.).

Rope, *t'hoqi, t'hoqe* (G. *t'hoci).*

Rose (Rosa sp.), *quari* (G. *vardi).*

Rosy-faced, *p'herish* (G., cf. colour).

Rotten, *mekvre.*

Round, circular, *quabai, girgold, murgvel, myrgual* (G.
    mrgvali);

round about, *metzkhep'he.*

Row, series, *tzkwer.*

Ruin, destruction, *khatsa, akra;* ruin (building), *merghve.*

Run (to), *lichvme, lichume, lint;* to run away, *liched.*

Rye, *manash* (winter rye), *kale, kul* (summer rye).

S

Sack, *dsadsra.*

Sacrifice (to), *lilgeni*; sacrifice, *lalgena, qvizh.*

Sad (to be), *litskue.*

Saddle, *hungir* (G. unagiri), *kekh*; pack-saddle, kap'h; to
saddle, *lihingre, zhilihungiri*

Salt, *dchim*; salted, *lydjim.*

Saltpetre, *quardshilá* (cf. *gvardjila*).

Sand, *kuishau kvishe* (G. *kvisha*); sandy, *kvishar.*

Satiated, *bamzar, mubiz.*

Saturday, *Sabt'hin, Sap'htin, Samtin.*

Save (to), *lished.*

Saw, file, *krerkh* (G.)

Say (to), *liqvisg, likvisg*; you told me, *maqved*; I say,
chuideh: he said, *lakhekun, qalaqv* (G.), *qakhaqv,
laqv, khaqv*; let him say, *khaqves*; what hast thou to
say? *ma dchughs leqvisg?* Scabbard, *ncrcldch.* Scarcely,
twFn.

Scatter (to), throw, *lishte, lishde, ligvrimbe.*

Scissors, *t'hurked, t'hrkiad, turlcate* (G. *macrateli*).

Screw, *dchakhrak* (G. *khrakhnili*).

Scythe, *merchil.*

Sea, *dzughva,* (G. *zghva*).

Seal, *beched* (G.).

Secretly, *ukba, uukbad, lyupzhunad, ushdvind, ruqhad.*

See (to), *litzed*; 1 saw, *amad*; thou sawest, *dchidjva, adjad*;
he

   saw, *akhad, naukhe* (G. *nakhva*).

Seed, *lashi.*

Seek (to), *lat'hkhel, lit'hkheli.*

Seize (to), *lirmi*; they caught, seized him, *adirmkh.*

Seldom, *merkhald.*

Sell (to), *lifsi, lihfdi*; to sell dear, *lihvdi dzvird* (G.); to sell cheap, *lihvdi iep'hd* (G.).

Send (to), *lizzi* lit'hone; he sent, *kavadzuze, kadzuze, adzuze*; send them here ! (sing.), *at'hzuz*

September, *Mykakh.*

Sermon, *qadag* (G. *kadageba*).

Serpent, *uidch, uidcheb, uidchelu, vidch, hertsem, vich, hich.*

Servant, *moznan, p'hamli* (? famulus), *momsakhvir* (G. *mosamsakhure*); travelling servant, *moyakhl*; maidservant, *moakhl* (G.).

Serve (to), *limsakhvre* (G.), *lisip*; I serve, *khvemsakhvre* (G.). Seven, *tshgvid* (G. *shvidi*).

Sew (to), *lishkhbi, zhilishkhbi.*

Shadow, shade, *mahera* (? chimera), *mahvera.*

Shaft of a cart, *markhil* (Arab., G. *markhili*, sledge).

Shame, *shguir* (G. *sirtzkhvili*).

Sharp, *skyre.*

Shave (to) (act.), *litsburi*; shaven, *lutsbure.*

Sheaf, *lenchver* (G. *mdcheleuli*).

Sheath, *uerchkh.*

Shed, *keshy.*

Sheep (ram), *oliak, gholaka, ghveliak*; (ewe), *gits.*

Sheepskin coat, *keesh.*

Shelter, *sadgem, sadgomi, sadguem* (G.), *lagna.*

Shepherd, *muldegh, andav.*

Shining, brilliant, *mykyre*

Shirt, *p'hatan*.

Shoes, *ber, chap'hul;* bast shoe, *dchabr* (cf. boots).

Shoot (to), *mat'hkuep'hi, lit'hveph* (cf. gun).

Shore, *pitu, dzgid* (G. *cide*).

Short, *mekvshde*.

Shoulder, *bardj, bardchili, lagleash;* shoulder-blade, *liniqan, bardjial*.

Shout, cry, *kil* (G.).

Shovel, *berg, bergied, laghir, lakhir, laukhe, nichaph* (G. *nichabi);*

to shovel snow from the roof, *lilghahi.* Shut (to), *linkhuemi*.

Sickle, *nashtak, nashtk*.

Sickness, *lizge* (cf. disease).

Side, *t'hqeb, lesg* (ribs); from that side, *echkhen;* from this side,

amkhen; on that side, *echkhan*. Silent (to be), *lichume* (G.), *likutse*.

Silk, *qadch*.

Silver, *vorchkhil* (G. *vertskhli);* silversmith, *varchkhili mishkid;*

made of silver, *varchkhilish, tsqenlish*.

Sin, *tsodv* (G.), *tsod,* pl. *tsodar*.

Sing, *lighral* (cf. play).

Sister, *dachvir,* pl. *dadchura, udil,* pi. *lavdila* (cf. G. *da*).

Sister-in-law (daughter-in-law), *t'he;ghra,* pl. *lat'helghra*.

Sit (to), *lisgure, lisqvre, zhilisqvre;* sit down! (pl.), *chesgurdal;* he was sitting down, *lakhsgurda;* he sat down, *zhilakhsgurda;* mounted man, *lalsgura*.

Six, *usqua, usgua, usgva* (G. *ekvsi*).

Sixty, *uusgvashd, vusgvaahd.*

Skin, hide, *t'huph, tup'h (gvare), kesh.*

Skinny, thin, *djaghm.*

Skirt, *kalt'ha* (G.).

Skull, *t'hkhvimi haqar.*

Sky, *detz, deg.*

Slab of stone, *sbendik.*

Slave, *p'hamli* (cf. Lat. famulus), *glekh* (G.) (cf. servant).

Sledge, *sau, sava, sav* (cf. lluss. *sani*).

Sleep, *uzh*; sleepy, *makduar*; to sleep, *livzhe*; to put to sleep,
    livzhune (vzh in the verb is *uzh* in the
noun). Sleeve, *dchvenezh.*

Slip (to), *ligeb, lizert.*

Slipper, *koshul.*

Slope of a mountain, *p'hap'hal* (cf. ascent).

Slowly, *tsqnard* (G.), *t'hamashd.*

Small, fine, *netsin* (? G. *nazi*), *khokhra.*

Smallpox, *mughvai, bogir*; pock-marked, *namghavar, nabgvir*
    (*mughvai,* flowers, so in G. flowers and smallpox are
    both *khvavilni).*

Smell, odour, *qvin, kuin* (cf. soul); to smell, *likhane* ; there
was
    a smell of, *lamkanda.*

Smith, *mushkid*; smithy, *lashkdash.*

Smoke, *kuam* (G. *cvamli)*; to smoke (of a chimney),
likuami;
    to smoke tobacco, *t'hut'huni lit'hre* (i.e. to
drink). Snaffle, *heghvir.*

Sneeze (to), *lichchkhune.*

Snore (to), *likhyrtune, lit'kholi.*

Snow, *mus*, dim. *musuld, shtur*; snowstorm, *kuse* (? also snowdrift); frozen snow, *hol* (cf. ice); to snow, *lishdve*; it is snowing, *shduve*; to make a road in the snow, *lichabi*; snowshoes, *tkilmare*.

Snub-nosed, *bant'ha*.

So much, *adjzum, amzum, cchsheld* (cf. number).

Socks, *kheral*.

Sofa, *lurgim* (cf. couch and for root, round).

Soft, *menshgve, menshgvar*.

Sole of foot or boot, *ghokerid*.

Solid, durable, *p'harsag*.

Somebody, *darghal, er, ere, iarvale*.

Something, *mezesir, imvale, male, uvma*.

Sometimes, *esesiny, esesin, khucai dinas* (cf. much).

Son, *gezal* (adult), *bep'hsh* (boy); adopted son, *gezald lugne;* son-in-law, *chizhe*, pl. *chizhal* and *lachzha*.

Song, *lighral* (G. *simghera*) (cf. play and sing), *lagral*.

Sorcerer, *qad* (cf. medicine man).

Soul, (*qvin, kuin* (cf. smell; in Mingrelian *shuri* has also this double sense).

Sour, *zhav* (G. *mzhave*), *mokhim* (G. *tsmakhi*).

Sow (to), *lilashi* (cf. seed).

Sow, *nezv, nezu* (G.).

Span, *kamin* (cf. hand).

Sparrow, *quinch*.

Speak (to), say, *limbavi, linbwal, ligurgali, lirgad* (cf. say) (cf. G. *ambavi*); speak! say ! (sing.), *khonubav*.

Spend (to), *likhirdjavi* (G.), *likhmari*; to squander, *libake*. Spider, *op'hop'hai* (in G. *oboba*, hoopoe).

Spirit, *qvin* (cf. soul).

Spirits, liquor, *harag* (G.).

Spit (for cooking), *shampuiur* (G.)

Spit (to), *litbyne*; to spit upon, *khatbuna*.

Spoil (to), damage, *lirashvi*.

Spoon, *kis* (G. *kovzi*).

Spring, fountain, *mazuab, viazvab, sarak (kved)*.

Springtime, *lup'hkhv, kamlizal*.

Spur, *des* (G. *dezi*).

Staff, stick, club, *lakht*; ironshod staff, *midchvra* (cf. alpenstock).

Stag, *lachu, lachv*.

Stammerer, *bekrai* (G. *brgu, brgvili*).

Stand (to), *ligne*; standing, *megne*; I stand, *mi khvag*; thou standest, *si khag*; he stands, *adcha khag*.

Star, *ant'hkhuask* (G. *varscvlavi*), *antqvsga, antqvasg*.

Starling, *parpand*.

Stay (to), *lised* (cf. remain).

Steal (to), *likvt'her*; they stole, *t'hkuithkh*.

Steel, *p'holad* (G.).

Steel for striking fire, *mort'hav, lakhach, lakech*.

Steep, *kach, tsap'hkh*.

Stern, severe, *mukhdji*.

Stick, *p'hawu, phavu*.

Stinking, *mukvnia* (cf. smell).

Stirrup, *avzhand, abzhand* (G. *avzhanda*).

Stocking (of cloth), *ber* (cf. shoe).

Stomach, *madchik*.

Stone, *bach, lurn, mukokh*; big stone, boulder, *gurna* (cf. granite); white stone, *mugkhu*; stony, *bachaar*.

Stool (three-legged), *bodchg*.

Store, provision, *khordchi* (G.), *leziz.*

Storm, *maota, bikhv.*

Story-teller, narrator, *membualdu* (cf. speak).

Straight, direct (adv.), *metsvind.*

Straw, *chal* (G.), *part.*

Strawberry, *basq.*

Strength, *khamsha.*

Stretch (to), *ligt'hkhune, libit*; stretched, *lugzune*; in order to stretch, *lagt'hkhunad.*

Strike (to), *likulp'hi*; I strike, *qaliqulp'hi*; he struck, *kakhakhud.*

Stroke, *naqer* (G.).

Strong, *badagi, lokmash, lykhmash, magar* (G.), *bygi.*

Stump, *bik.*

Stupid, *udjkviv* (G. *uchkuo*); stupidity, *umbazh, udchkviv* (cf. wit).

Succeed (to); he succeeded, *adjisr.*

Such, *amguar* (G.).

Suck (to), *litssdani*; suckling, *isgamechem.*

Suddenly, *esnar.*

Suffer (to), *lit'hmine* (G.).

Suffice (to), *liri*; it will be enough for us, *qagvar.*

Sugar, *shakar* (G.).

Suit (to), *limarg.*

Sulphur, *gogir* (G. *gogirdi*).

Summer, *zai, amzav* (cf. year).

Summit, *t'hkhum* (cf. head), *kvindchil.*

Sun, *muzh, mizh* (G. *mze*), *?mlok* sunlight, *mizhi narhi, mizhimnarhi*; sunrise, *mizhi lakhad, mizhi latsad*;

sunset, *mizhi lahar, mizhi laz*; eclipse of the sun, *mizhi libure.*

Sunday, *Mishladeg* (cf. sun and day).

Superfluous, *masar, nametan* (G.).

Supper, *vakhsham* (G.).

Surprised (to be), *liskvrale*; he was surprised, *at'hsakvralunda.*

Surround (to), *litskhep'h;* to be surrounded, *litskhap'h*; he surrounded, *akhtskhep'ha.*

Suspect (to), *librali* (G.).

Svanetia, *Shvan*; Svanetian, *Mushir, Mushvni*; native of Svanetia, *mushvan.*

Swallow, *shdaval.*

Swallow (to), *lirtqvi.*

Sweet, *mudchkhvi, khoja gömasch* (i.e. good taste).

Swelling, tumour, *myskir.*

Swiftness, *lynchkar* (G.).

Swim (to), *litzrevi.*

Sword, *dashna*, dim. *dashnil* (G.), *khmal* (G.); hilt, *midchv;* blade, *berezh* (cf. iron); edge, *uishkv.*

T

Table, *tabag* (G.); round table with three legs, *p'hichk*; tablecloth, *chithish tabag.*

Tail, *hakved, hakvad.*

Take (to), *liked, lipshe, li, libishd*; let us take, *lelkuded*; he took, *enie, adie*; take! (sing.), *atkha*; to take out, *lishgvne, litkhe*; they took out, *it'hkhekh*; to take away, *likhi, light;* he took away, *emkhin*; to take off, *likche, likedi*; he took off, *chokhokida.*

Tall, *khocha tanish* (cf. great and *tani* G., form).

Tape, ribbon, *suinai* (G. *zonari).*

Tar, *p'hise* (G. *p'hisi).*

Tea, *chain* (G. *chai).*

Teach (to), *lit'hvri* (cf. pupil); teacher, *mat'hvri.*

Tear, *kum*, pi. *kumrar, kim*; to shed (throw) tears, *likvane.*

Tear off (to), *litqvp'he.*

Teat, nipple, *lus, lyus, dudul* (G. *dzudzu).*

Telescope, spyglass, *milionka, milyuen.*

Tell (to), say, *liqvisg, limbui, likiadi* (cf. say, speak); tell me! *mekvt'h, gvebt'h* (sing.), *akhambuet'h* (pl.); they told, *kokhumbavekh*; you told me, *maqved*; he will tell thee, *dcheqvni.*

Temple (of the head), *laghachir.*

Ten, *eshd.*

Tether (to), *libem* (G. *bma,* to hind); the tethered horse broke

loose, *lube chazhd anqvits*; he is tethered, *khab.* Thank (to), *likhuami.*

Thankful (to be), *libazh* ; ho will be grateful, *khebzhi.*

That (dom.), *edchi* (G. *ese*).

Thaw (to), melt, *lipzhune*.

Then, at that time, *eurdiser, echka, echkas, achqa*.

Thence, *echon, echkhan*.

There, *chuqhal, echichu, eche* (a long way off), *echa, echau,*
    echkhe, echechvin (near at hand).

They, *(idjiar, edjiar, min;* their, *adjiaresh* ; them, *mine*.

Thick, *skel* (G. *skeli*).

Thief, *kvit'h*.

Thigh, *p'hoq*.

Thimble, *sat'hat'hr* (G. *sat'hit'huri*) (cf. finger).

Thin, *netsin* (cf. small), *dotchöl*; to grow thin, *chulichkhep'h,*
    liehkhep'h; I have grow thin, *chvochkhap'h*.

Think (to), *lichne, lichkvari*; they thought, *esehinekh* ; let him

    not think! *garesen*. Third, *mesma* (G. *mesame*).

Thirst, *map'hun;* to thirst, *lip'hne*; thirsty, *ubza*.

This, *al, ali, ala, ale, am, ami* (G.).

Thither, *enqad, echad* (a long way oft), *echkhav* (near at hand),
    echkhan.

 Thorn, *tzaq*.

Thou, *si*.

Thought, opinion, mind *(azri* G.), *saazr*.

Thread, *kip, kip'h* (see rib).

Threaten (to), *likhuznal*.

Three, *semi* (G. *sami*); thrice, *samdchel* (G.).

Threshing-floor, *kevr, kiavir, kal;* to thresh, *liklavi*.

Throat, *qinchkh, qia* (G. *qeli*), *kharkh* (G. *qarqanto*).

Through, *lisqa*.

Throw (to), *likvane, liqvane, lip'hshtva, lishde, likvri*; he
   threw, *adkvar, akhp'husht*; I shall throw, *ot'hqrane,*
   thrown, *meshde.*

Thrust in (to), *lidzgrin, litzqere.*

Thunder, to thunder, *lirkhunal*; lightning, *meqh* (G *mekhi*).

Thursday, *Tsash, Tzaash.*

Thus, *adjzhin, adjzhi, ash, esh* (G. *aset'hi*).

Thy, *isgu, iskvu, isgui, isgua, isguau, isgvy.*

Tick (insect), *dchghibar.*

Time, *drev, dvrev* (G. *droeba*), *ona, khan* (G.).

Tin, *kaliai (? Gallia)* (G. *cala*).

Tinder, *hobed* (G. *abedi*).

Tired (to be), *lip'hash.*

To, at, *tsakhan* (suffix).

Tobacco, *t'hut'hni, t'hut'hyn.*

To-day, *ladi, ladghi* (cf. day).

Toe (see finger).

Together, *ashklivd*; we went together, *na ashkhvd
ochadd.*

To-morrow, *mukhar, makhar, mkhar*; day after
tomorrow,
   mykhar echkhan (cf. thence).

Tongue, *nin* (G. *ena*).

To-night, *bazi.*

Too much, *suru.*

Tooth, *sht'huq, shduk, shtig*; molar, *lelygvi* (cf. heart);
   toothache, *shtyqre mazig* (cf. disease).

Touch (to), *libik,   lip'hde.*

Towel, *lakvtzan, pirsakhots* (G.).

Tower, *murqram, murkma, muqvam, qoshqi* (Turk.).

Town, *kalak* (G.).

Trace, track, *nazu.*

Trade (to), *lighvchari* (G. *vajari*, merchant).

Transform (to), *lispe.*

Translate (to), interpret, *lit'hirgmani* (G. *targmna*).

Tree, *megam, meghiam*; trunk, *dchirk.*

Tribe, *t'hem* (G. *t'homi*).

Tripod, three-legged stool, *bodchg.*

Trouble (to), *lip'hesh;* do not trouble thyself, *nun p'hcsheni;* do not trouble yourselves, *nom p'heshnid.*

Trough, *sargil* (? root, *rg*, cf. round).

Trousers, *sakhshur, sakhshvir.*

Truth, *samtsun*; in truth, really, *tkitzd*; it is true, *samtzvind.* Tuesday, *thagash, thakhcsh, t'hakhat.*

Tumbler (wooden), *kat'hkh, p'haken.*

Tumour, swelling, *myshy* (cf. swelling).

"Tur" *(Aegoceros Pallasii)*, *ghvash, ghuash, vasher, qvitsra.*

Turkey-cock, *qyrna, quich*; turkey-hen, *qyrma kat'hal.*

Turn (to) (intr.), *lisip.*

Tusk, *kil, lelgui* (cf. tooth, molar).

Twelve, *ieshtieru, eskdyervi.*

Twenty, *yarveslid.*

Twist (to), *litsurkhi, lispune.*

Two, *ieri, yervi* (G. *ori*).

U

Uncle (on father's side), *buba;* (on mother's side), *pidzai.*

Under, underneath, *chuqa, chukvan, ckubal.*

Undying, *udgara* (cf. die).

Unexpectedly, *t'hei.*

Unhappy, *sabral* (G.), *sabrila, sabrala, ubdvir* (G. *ubeduri).* Universe, *kveqana* (G.); universal, *abuasti.*

Unpleasant, *maidchale* (cf. ? *maid,* hunger).

Unripe, *ugka, uka.*

Unsuitable, it is unsuitable, *mat'hkhaqa* (? cf. not and necessary)

Until, *echkad, vod.*

Up, *zhibav, zhikan.*

Upon, *lokhkvem.*

Upper, *zhibe;* upper floor, *darbaz* (G.).

Upright, *kach* (on end).

Urine, *nasen.*

Useful (to be), *limkakhal;* useful, *sargeb* (G.).

Useless, in vain, *ughuri, tsvidd.*

Ushkulian (native of Ushkul), *Muvshgvil.*

V

Vain (in), to no purpose, *tsvidd* (G. *tsudad*); vain chatter,
    tsvidi mugurgali (cf. speak).

Valley, *mindori* (G.).

Variegated, *chirel* (G.).

Vein, *dsarghual* (G. *dzarghvi*).

Velvet, *khaverd* (G.).

Very, *gun, gunu, suru* (cf. too much), *mawar, mevar.*

Victory, *litsre.*

Village, *sop'hel* (G.); village green, *sup'h, svip'h* ; member of
    village council of twelve, *mybari.*

Vine, *vaz* (G.); vineyard, *menakh* (G. *venakki)*; grapes,
    qurdzen (G.).

Viuegar, *dzmar* (G.).

Voice, *tqbip'h* (cf. noise), *her.*

Vomiting, *lishkhune.*

W

Wail, lamentation, *zar* (G. and Pers.).

Waist, *lartqa* (cf. girdle).

Wait (to), *lidranal, lighli, lighalve;* ho waits, *khedranal;* he waited, *ighalva.*

Wake up (to) (intr.), *litskhne, litskhine, lietzkh;* they woke (themselves) up, *t'hotskhastakh;* to wake up (trans.), rouse, *litzkhune.*

Walk (to), *lizelal, izelal, lezna;* walking, *mezalal.*

Wall, *chvad.*

Walnut (*Juglans regia*), *gak, kak* (G. *kakali*).

Want (to), wish : I want, *mitzga.*

War, *lashkrianob* (G.) (cf. army); warrior, *lamargiash.*

Warm, *tebdi* (G.).

Wash (to), oneself, *libral, labral;* ho was washing him.solf, *ibralda;* to wash clothes, *lishqvdi.*

Wasp, *bizik.*

Watchman, guard, *melcha, qarvil* (G. *qaraul*).

Water, *lits, nits* (cf. river); to bring water, *liltsi;* water running through a trough or conduit, *sarag* (cf. spring); mineral water, *skim, sgimer;* to water, *lit'hvne;* w'ater-carrier, *myltsi;* waterfall, *mach, khap'h* (G.); water-jug, *vokhar.*

Wax, *djvid.*

We, *na, nai.*

Weak, *umbets;* weakness, *listve.*

Wealth, *qet'hil* (G. *ketili,* good), *lymdidre* (G. *simdidre*).

Weapons, *havedch, iaraghi* (G.) (cf. arms).

Weather, *dar* (G.); good weather, *khocha dar*; bad weather, *khola dar*.

Wedding, *qortzil, kvertsil* (G.).

Wedge, *t'hal*.

Wednesday, *dchimash*.

Week, *nagzi, nagza*.

Weep (to), *ligvni*, I weep, *khvigvni*; he weeps, *igvni*.

Weigh (to), *litsni* (G.).

Well, *khochamd* (cf. good).

West, *lekva, dasavlet'h* (O.); westward, *lakva*.

Wet, *zyski*; to wet, *lizhre*; moist, moisture, *myzhir*.

What, *ma* (G. *ra*), *mai, mayhal, maroq, im*; what art thou doing? *im khicho?*

Wheat, *kuetsen, quetzen, diar* (bread); winter wheat, *namzhghor*.

Wheel, *barbeld*.

When, *zhilakh, shoma, lakh, lakhasa*.

Whence, *iman, imkhan*.

Where, *imeg, imegue, imeva, ime*.

Whetstone, *lasheer*.

Whey, *tsak*.

Which, *kheda*.

Whilst, *zhi* (as suffix to verbal noun).

Whip, *mudrakh, madrag* (G. *matrakhi*).

White, *t'het'hne, t'het'hna, t'heet'hvne* (G. *t'het'hri*); white stone, *mugkhu*; whitish, *mot'ht'hwan*; whiter, *khot'ht'hwana*; whitest, *mat'ht'hwana*.

Whither, *imav, imt'he*.

Who, *iar;* to whom, *ias;* whose, *isha*.

Whortleberry (*Vaccinium myrtillus*), *melguma* (*Vaccinium arctostaphylos*), *tzinka*.

Why, *ma, imgha, imghai, imghesir,* why not, *kaighadom.*

Wide, *lygan, masheri;* to widen, stretch, *limshari;* widened, *lumshare.*

Widow (to become a), *likvrive* (G.).

Wife, *khekhv, iekhul, ikhvt, ekhvt, oeh;* wives, *lalukhva;* house of wife's family, *lamtil.*

Willow *(Salix sp.),* *bagura* (the tall broad-leaved variety), *gynchish* (bush).

Wind, *bikv* (cf. storm), *biyk, biklo.*

Window, *lakvra, lalchwra, lakhura, sennai.*

Wine, *ghvinal, ghuine, ghuinol* (G. *ghvino*); wine-cellar, *kets;* Eucharistic wine, *zedash.*

Winter, *lint'hv, amlint'hv.*

Wish, desire, *hadv;* to wish, *likved;* I wish, *gvimar* (cf. have and heart) ; I do not wish, *mamaqu;* thou wishest, *djaku;* thou wishedst, *dchekuad;* they wish, *khakud.* I wish, *mi maku;* thou wishest, *si dchaku;* he wishes, *achas khaku.*

Wit, intelligence, *bazh, dchkuiv* (G. *dchkua*), *tqel.*

Witch, *gudmetsar.*

Without, *u* as prefix and *ad* as suffix, e.g. *udiarad,* without bread.

Wolf, *thkhere, thkherem, thkhare, thkhcril.*

Woman, *zural.*

Wood, forest, *tzkhek* (G. *tqe*); wood, firewood, *zek;* wooden,
zekish, megmemish (cf. tree).

Woodpecker, *muqune, maqguna.*

Wool, *matq* (G. *matqli)*; woollen cloth, *shart'hkvin.*

Word, *naku.*

Work, *limshai* (G. *mushaoba)*, *ligirdje*; to work, *limshiel.*

World, *qveqana* (G.).

Worm, *myt* (G. *matli).*

Worthless, *leg* (cf. bad).

Wound, *lyqiach*; to wound, *likcheni*; wounded, *lukach*; he
wounded, *chadkache.*

Wrath, *riskhv* (G.).

Wrinkled, *lukhudche.*

Wrist, *mekhra.*

Write (to), *liri* (cf. book).

Y

Yard, farmyard, courtyard, *hazv, haz* (G. *ezo), sup'hil*; churchyard, *sasp'hlav* (G.).

Yawn (to), *likshiel.*

Year, *za, zai, zau* (cf. summer).

Yellow, *qvit'hel* (G.).

Yes, *adu, ho* (G.).

Yesterday, *lat'h*; day before yesterday, *sguebi ladegh* (cf. day).

Yield (to), *liqekh.*

Yoke, *ughva* (G. *ugheli).*

You, *sga, sgiai*; your, *isgvei.*

Young, *makhe, ghvazhi* (G. *vazhi*); younger, *khokhra, maghrene*; young man, *makhe vazh.*

www.ingramcontent.com/pod-product-compliance
Lightning Source LLC
Chambersburg PA
CBHW060449160726
47992CB00003B/1140